CW01664456

A LIFEBUILDER BIBLE STUDY

ESTHER

Character Under Pressure

9 Studies
for individuals or groups

Patty Pell

With Notes for Leaders

SCRIPTURE UNION
207–209 QUEENSWAY, BLETCHLEY
MILTON KEYNES, BUCKINGHAMSHIRE (UK), MK2 2EB

©1995 by Patty Pell

First published in the United States by InterVarsity Press.
First published in Great Britain by Scripture Union, 1995.

All rights reserved. No part of this book may be reproduced, stored in a retrieval system, or transmitted, in any form or by any means, electronic, mechanical, photocopying, recording or otherwise, without the prior permission of Scripture Union.

Unless otherwise indicated, Scripture quotations are taken from the HOLY BIBLE, NEW INTERNATIONAL VERSION. Copyright © 1973, 1978, 1984 by International Bible Society. Anglicisation copyright © 1979, 1984, 1989. Used by permission of Hodder and Stoughton Limited.

Cover photograph: Dennis Frates

ISBN 0 86201 996 6

Printed in England by Ebenezer Baylis & Son Limited, The Trinity Press, Worcester and London

Contents

Getting the Most from LifeBuilder Bible Studies

Many of us long to fill our minds and our lives with Scripture. We desire to be transformed by its message. LifeBuilder Bible Studies are designed to be an exciting and challenging way to do just that. Their ultimate goal is to help us build our lives on God's Word.

How They Work

LifeBuilder Bible Studies have a number of distinctive features. Perhaps the most important is that they are *inductive* rather than *deductive*. In other words, they lead us to *discover* what the Bible says rather than simply *telling* us what it says.

They are also thought provoking. They help us to think about the meaning of the passage so that we can truly understand what the author is saying. The questions require more than one-word answers.

The studies are personal. Questions expose us to the promises, assurances, exhortations and challenges of God's Word. They are designed to allow the Scriptures to renew our minds so that we can be transformed by the Spirit of God. This is the ultimate goal of all Bible study.

The studies are versatile. They are designed for student, neighbourhood and church groups. They are also effective for individual study.

How They're Put Together

LifeBuilder Bible Studies also have a distinctive format. Each study need take no more than forty-five minutes in a group setting or thirty minutes in a personal study – unless you choose to take more time.

The studies can be used within a quarter system in a church and fit well in a semester or trimester system on a college campus. If a guide has more than thirteen studies, it is divided into two or occasionally three parts of approximately twelve studies each.

LifeBuilder Bible Studies use a workbook format. Space is provided for writing answers to each question. This is ideal for personal study and allows group members to prepare in advance for the discussion.

The studies also contain leader's notes. They show how to lead a group discussion, provide additional background information on certain questions, give helpful tips on group dynamics and suggest ways to deal with problems which may arise during the discussion. With such helps, someone with little or no experience can lead an effective study.

Suggestions for Individual Study

1. As you begin each study, pray that God will help you to understand and apply the passage to your life.

2. Read and reread the assigned Bible passage to familiarize yourself with what the author is saying. In the case of book studies, you may want to read through the entire book prior to the first study. This will give you a helpful overview of its contents.

3. A good modern translation of the Bible, rather than the King James Version or a paraphrase, will give you the most help. The New International Version, the New American Standard Bible and the Revised Standard Version are all recommended. However, the questions in this guide are based on the New International Version.

4. Write your answers in the space provided in the study guide. This will help you to express your understanding of the passage clearly.

5. It might be good to have a Bible dictionary handy. Use it to look up any unfamiliar words, names or places.

Suggestions for Group Study

1. Come to the study prepared. Follow the suggestions for individual study mentioned above. You will find that careful preparation will greatly enrich your time spent in group discussion.

2. Be willing to participate in the discussion. The leader of your group will not be lecturing. Instead, he or she will be encouraging the members of the group to discuss what they have learned from the passage. The leader will be asking the questions that are found in this guide. Plan to share what God has taught you in your individual study.

3. Stick to the passage being studied. Your answers should be based on the verses which are the focus of the discussion and not on outside authorities such as commentaries or speakers. This guide deliberately avoids jumping

from book to book or passage to passage. Each study focuses on only one passage. Book studies are generally designed to lead you through the book in the order in which it was written. This will help you follow the author's argument.

4. Be sensitive to the other members of the group. Listen attentively when they share what they have learned. You may be surprised by their insights! Link what you say to the comments of others so the group stays on the topic. Also, be affirming whenever you can. This will encourage some of the more hesitant members of the group to participate.

5. Be careful not to dominate the discussion. We are sometimes so eager to share what we have learned that we leave too little opportunity for others to respond. By all means participate! But allow others to also.

6. Expect God to teach you through the passage being discussed and through the other members of the group. Pray that you will have an enjoyable and profitable time together.

7. If you are the discussion leader, you will find additional suggestions and helpful ideas for each study in the leader's notes. These are found at the back of the guide.

Introducing Esther

"Just Do It" has been a successful and popular slogan the past few years for the athletic company Nike. It refers to getting in shape and participating in athletics no matter what the physical or mental strain. But the slogan brings something else to my mind after spending time in the book of Esther: it reminds me to *just do it*—just do the right thing no matter what the consequences.

In the book of Esther we see the lives of several characters played out. There are those people who are selfish and prideful, seeking only personal recognition, and there are those who risk everything for others and choose integrity in the face of great opposition. Esther is a book about developing godly character. In the midst of a culture which does not emphasize doing what is right, this book speaks to us in profound ways.

As we read through the events of Esther, we are given a description of what godly character is and what it is not. But there is another very strong theme that weaves in and around the theme of character. It is the idea that God is working in the circumstances and events of people's lives to bring about his plans. God is the director, the conductor, the weaver. As God works in our lives, we must choose what is right so that we can be a part of God's plan.

The events of this powerful book take place in Persia during the reign of King Xerxes from 486 to 465 B.C. It has been over one hundred years since the beginning of the exile, and some Jews have returned to Jerusalem. The story is set in the city of Susa, which is where the king has his winter palace. It involves the whole of the Jewish people, but revolves around the lives of King Xerxes, Esther, her uncle,

Mordecai, and Haman, the king's highest noble.

Esther's story presents the last major threat to the Jewish people in the Old Testament period. The threat and the Jews' deliverance is recorded in this book. The Jewish festival of Purim, which is still celebrated today, is established in Esther, which accounts for the book's great popularity among the Jewish people. It is a wonderful story of God's providence and the character of his people told with humor, irony, repetition and contrast.

Esther will stir us to examine our character, the deep aspects of our hearts. It will encourage us in taking a stand for what is right and give us courage that God is still in control. It is a book that we need to study so that we can glorify God with our whole being and begin to be witnesses in our world because of our integrity. If we allow the themes of Esther to penetrate our lives, we will begin to stop and question our actions and thoughts and align them with God's desire.

May your study in Esther produce in you a longing for consistent godly character.

1
A Little Respect

Esther 1

One of my favorite and most influential teachers was a high-school English teacher. His class was extremely difficult and challenging, but I loved it and worked diligently in order to do well. The reason I respected this teacher so much is that he listened to me and valued me.

We would all like to be respected by others, and so we try many ways of gaining that respect. Some try to gain it through controlling others or by demanding it. However, one of the ways respect is gained is by appreciating others and showing them respect.

---

1. Think of one person whom you respect. Describe some characteristics of this person and what he or she did to gain your respect.

Father – fair & honest

---

2. Read chapter 1. Who are the people we encounter in this first chapter? King Xerxes Queen Vashti

Courtiers etc. wives noblemen

3. Describe the celebration given by King Xerxes (vv. 2-8).

Banquet ~~Feasting~~ for all from least to greatest

Why might the king have given such an extravagant party?

---

4. Why does King Xerxes ask Queen Vashti to come to him (vv. 10-11)?

To show ~~her~~ off her beauty to the nobles

---

5. The king's request places Vashti in a difficult position. What factors would she have been weighing in her decision (v. 12)?

That the King was drunk + they would all ogle her degrading
The King would be angry + let down in front of his people.

---

6. What can we observe about King Xerxes' character so far?

He is a show off and wants his own way. Women are inferior to the males. Proud selfish

---

7. Think of a time when you were placed in a difficult situation. What was your response?

8. Why did the wise men perceive Queen Vashti's refusal to be so dangerous to the kingdom (vv. 16-20)?

Because all the women would feel that they could disobey their husbands

9. The wise men mention respect several times in this chapter. In their view how was respect gained and maintained?

By fear of ~~what~~ them – demanded

10. How does respect actually develop between people?

By love, kindness understanding Trust. mutual regard & appreciation esteem consideration & honor (dictionary - respect)

11. In what ways can you show appreciation and regard to those around you?

Giving them time & encouragement

12. Describe one thing that you can do this week to show someone respect.

2
Trusting God's Work

Esther 2

When the curtain rises and the play begins, we see and hear the actors and actresses tell a story. But the most important person in the play is not on the stage. The director is the one who has instructed the cast for months before on where to stand and sit and when and how to say a line. The director is behind the scenes giving final instructions, touching up makeup and encouraging the players. The play is a success because of the director, who has orchestrated every detail of the play.

In the book of Esther God is not mentioned, but he is the key figure in the story. He works through the circumstances to place everything in order so that his plans will be accomplished. God is the director of our lives as well. He puts all the pieces in just the right places and knits everything together. As we look back at different times in our lives, we can see his handprints all over. Our response to him is to look for his hand moving and to trust his direction.

---

1. Describe a time in your past when you saw God work through circumstances in your life to bring something about.

To join a Housegroup – Nicki

4 years since Vashti's dethronement

2. Read chapter 2. Summarize the plan to find a new queen that King Xerxes put into action (vv. 1-4). All the beautiful ~~girls~~ virgins in the Province to be brought to the King's harem & placed under the King's Eunuch Hegai & be given beauty treatments for 12 months

3. How does Esther enter the story and become the queen (vv. 5-17)?

She is a beautiful girl & is taken to the harem & the King is so ~~pleased~~ attracted to her that he crowns her Queen.

4. Many young women were brought to the palace and placed in the harem. What was the role of these women and what were their lives like? Very dull - no rights, restricted They were all looked after & pampered & made beautiful to see if they would please the King for sexual pleasure

5. It is mentioned three times that Esther won approval in someone's eyes (vv. 9, 15, 17). What does this tell us about Esther?

She has more than just beauty - she has a certain presence & personality

6. Think of someone you know who finds favor with others because of that person's presence and personality. How can you begin living out one of the characteristics of this person in your own life?

Carolyn Pamela Raybourne

7. How would Esther's life, role and rights be different from the rest of the women in the harem when she became the queen?

More rights freedom influence & authority

8. How does Mordecai enter into the plot of the story (vv. 19-23)?

He is keeping an eye on Esther + comes to the palace each day. He tells of a plot to kill the King which he overhears

9. What does this glimpse of Mordecai's life tell us about his character?

He is honest caring & just integrity even in the face of danger

10. Even though God has not been directly mentioned in the book, where do you see his hand moving in the story so far?

Esthers beauty - Queen Vashti's refusal Modecai's employment at gate & his name & deed being recorded The people Esther meets

11. Where do you see God's hand moving in circumstances in your life right now?

How do you think he wants you to respond?

3
Evaluating Advice

Esther 3

"No man has any right to counsel others who is not ready to hear and follow the counsel of the Lord." This quote from A. W. Tozer reminds me of the responsibility we have in giving advice to others. It is a serious thing to give counsel, and it is also a serious step to take the counsel of our friends. So often we give quick advice to one another without truly understanding the situation or without pure motives. Part of godly character is knowing how to evaluate the advice we receive and in turn to offer sound and wise counsel.

---

1. When in your life have you received good advice and when have you received poor advice?

---

2. Read chapter 3. List all the words and phrases in this chapter which bring to mind tragedy or conflict.

not kneel down or pay honour

Review Conflict between Jews +

Amalekites Read 3 passages

3. What is the conflict between Haman and Mordecai which causes Haman's intense reaction to Mordecai (vv. 2-6)?

Amalakite & Jew not being honoured & refusing to obey commands.

4. How does Haman persuade the king to adopt his plan to destroy the Jews (vv. 8-9)? He gets round the King & offers his own money & tells of people in the kingdom who disobey him, the Jews were in fact obedient to the King & followed their own laws truths & half truths

5. At what point in your life have you been tempted to use half-truths and lies to convince someone?

What were you feeling at the time?

6. Describe the orders contained in the king's edict (v. 13).

destroy kill & annihilate all Jews young & old men & women & little children on the 13th day of the 12th month.

7. In verses 12-14 the words *each, every* and *all* are repeated frequently. What might the author have been trying to communicate in this detailed description of the edict? no one should be left out intensity of the threat which was overwhelming & all encompassing

8. What have we learned about Haman's character in this chapter?

Ruthless crafty hatred
Wanting to get his own way

9. This chapter gives us even more detail about who King Xerxes was. What do we learn about him? He is very pride full
& greedy Lack of concern or compassion
Sits down to drink while unconcerned
about the destruction he has ordered.

10. How might you guard against giving unwise advice?

We need to know the whole story
& not jump to quick conclusions
Remain humble - seek God's advice.

11. What are some ways you can evaluate the advice you receive from others? Seek the Lord's guidance
ask other peoples help. Our
group is a good example.
Make sure the advice you
take is sound & good.

4
Doing the Right Thing
Esther 4

Laszlo Tokes was a pastor in Timisoara, Romania, during the reign of Ceausescu under the communist regime. He had dedicated his life to bringing about revival in the church in Romania despite opposition and danger. He risked his life to preach the gospel and stand up against the communist government. Because of his courage and integrity he helped the people to win their freedom.

God places us in situations where he wants to use us, and in those situations we will be faced with the choice of doing what God calls us to do or doing what is against God. We may never face circumstances like those of Laszlo Tokes, but doing what is right includes little things: giving back extra change when a cashier makes a mistake or letting the cable company know about the free service that's been coming in. Whether the stakes are large or small, it takes the same character qualities of courage and moral strength to choose what is right.

---

1. Describe an instance where obeying God's call meant taking a risk or facing a difficulty.

2. Read chapter 4. What is the sequence of events?

---

3. Describe the response of Mordecai and the Jews to Haman's plot (vv. 1-3).

---

4. How does the fasting of the Jewish people in verse 3 contrast with parts of the first three chapters?

---

5. Why do you think Mordecai was so confident in his plan to stop the annihilation of the Jews (vv. 6-8)?

---

6. What is Esther's first reaction to Mordecai's request that she go to the king (vv. 9-11)?

---

7. What do you think Esther may have been feeling (vv. 9-11)?

8. Think back to the situation God called you to in which obeying meant facing great risks. What was your first reaction, and what were your feelings when God called you?

---

9. How do Mordecai's arguments in verses 12-14 persuade Esther to go to the king?

---

10. In this chapter how do we see God's sovereignty and people's responses working together?

---

11. What character qualities does Esther show in her response to Mordecai's second message?

---

12. Think of a present context in which God has placed you to do his will. What risks do you face in doing the right thing in this context?

What character qualities must you exhibit in order to do the right thing?

5
The Heart of the Matter

Esther 5

My schoolteacher husband came home one day from work with an unpleasant note from a parent. The note expressed anger and concern over his performance as a teacher. My husband was very wounded and puzzled by the note, but he made an appointment to meet with the parent the next day. In the face of a situation that could have led my husband to bitterness and anger I watched him respond with courage, compassion and humility. Because of his response the misunderstanding was clarified and the relationship was reconciled.

Our character comes through especially in times where we are facing a difficult task or situations or people that anger us. Our response to these kinds of occurrences in our life tells a great deal about our character. Do we face them with courage and humility or with anger, bitterness and pride? Esther faces her task with courage and dependence on God, while Haman is consumed with anger and hatred because of Mordecai. Both show the condition of their hearts.

---

1. What example comes to mind when you think of a person acting with courage or humility?

2. Read chapter 5. What risks does Esther take in verses 1-8?

Being killed & leaving her people without help. Not answering the King's question twice

3. What do you think Esther may have been feeling in verse 1?

Frightened alone hungry & weak

4. Look back at 4:15-16. What enabled Esther to face the risk of going to the king without being summoned? Through prayer the help of God - she could not do it alone - We all need help & support of friends & family to do God's will. Also the fact she had probably been put in the Palace for this specific purpose

5. How can the support of other believers be helpful to you in the midst of a trial you are going through now? Sharing - as we do here - Praying together

6. Esther asks the king and Haman to attend a banquet. What may have been the reason for such a request (vv. 4-8)? Prayer most important

She is giving to the King & not just asking for help & it would be easier not in the King's court - home ground

7. The second time the king asks Esther to make her request known, she answers him. What do her words reveal about her character (vv. 7-8)? humility Seeks to please & to honour the King

8. What characteristics do we see in Haman (vv. 9-14)?

Arrogant Anger bitterness + pride
Power + influence

9. Haman boasts about having everything: sons, wealth, position and recognition. Why do you think Haman is still so consumed with hatred for Mordecai? Hatred for Jews

10. How does the passage contrast Esther's character and Haman's character?

11. Where in your own life do you see the qualities of Esther and the qualities of Haman?

12. In what current situation can you try to respond with the courage and humility of Esther?

6
Recognizing Unrighteousness

Esther 6

When I take an honest look at myself, I see many ugly spots that mar my character. One of the ugliest traits is my desire to make myself look better than others. This ungodly character trait seeps into my relationships and damages intimacy. For each of us there are things about our character that are displeasing to God; perhaps it is pride or arrogance, selfish ambition or manipulation. Because we let those things grow in our lives rather than allowing God to remove them, we experience the various consequences of our unrighteousness.

---

1. What is one aspect of your character you would like to be more Christlike?

Forgiveness

---

2. Read chapter 6. What events in this chapter seem coincidental but lead to the development of the story?

The King waking/ Reading about Mordecai & Haman being in the Court

3. How does the king respond to discovering Mordecai's role in thwarting the assassination plot (vv. 2-6)? Asks him what he would do for the man the King delights to honour

4. Where do you see irony in King Xerxes' and Haman's actions on this particular night (vv. 1-6 and 5:14)? the King wanted to honour & Haman wanted to destroy M

5. God has been working quietly to bring together many of the incidents recorded in this chapter. He uses insignificant things to work out his plans. Tell about a time where God used an insignificant thing in your life for his purposes.

6. What else can we discern about Haman's character through his response to the king's question in verses 7-9? He thought it was for himself & wanted to show off to all the city

7. How might Haman have been feeling when he discovered that Mordecai, his enemy, is the one to be honored? humiliated frightened for his life

8. Haman sought comfort from his wife and friends after his ride through the city with Mordecai, but he receives a very different response. How do his wife and advisors interpret the situation and react to Haman (vv. 12-14)? Why? His wife feels he is beaten & his friends leave him

How do they seem to be distancing themselves from Haman?

---

9. How has the ungodliness in Haman's character led to his humiliation?

---

10. Think back to the characteristic in your life which is not always Christlike. What might be (or have been) some negative consequences of this trait?

---

11. What is one thing that you can do this week, with God's help, to reform your character?

7
Character No Matter What

Esther 7

This is what the wicked are like—
    always carefree, they increase in wealth.
Surely in vain have I kept my heart pure;
    in vain have I washed my hands in innocence. (Psalm 73:12-13)

These words express the struggle in the heart of the psalmist. He is wrestling because he does not see justice being carried out; instead, the wicked prosper and the righteous are plagued. In a similar way Esther and Mordecai have chosen to do what is right throughout the story, yet they face destruction. Haman, who is prideful, angry and bitter, has been successful in plotting against the Jews. Finally, in chapter 7 Esther and Mordecai see justice taking place. However, in our lives we do not always see justice when we choose to do what is right. The people of God must have consistent character whether or not justice prevails in this life.

---

1. Give an example of a situation in which justice was served.

2. Read chapter 7. Name all of the truths that were previously hidden but are now revealed in this chapter.

---

3. This chapter revolves around Queen Esther, King Xerxes and Haman. What might each of them be feeling at the beginning of the banquet?

---

4. How does Esther present her request (vv. 3-4)?

---

5. What thoughts and emotions might the king and Haman experience when Esther presents her request (vv. 6-7)?

---

6. What is ironic about the events of this banquet?

---

7. What do verses 6-8 reveal about Haman's character?

8. How do you see justice carried out in the lives of Esther, Mordecai and Haman?

---

9. What should be our motivation for doing what is right?

As Christians, when should we expect to see justice served and when should we be satisfied with doing what is right? Give examples from your experience.

---

11. How can you seek justice in a situation where you currently see injustice?

How will you respond if justice is not served?

8
Praising God's Faithfulness

Esther 8

As the sunshine filtered through the sanctuary windows, the pastor stood and asked for the congregation to share how God had been faithful. One by one the people rose to their feet. There were testimonies about marriages restored, physical healings, new passion for service, children coming to Christ and spiritual growth. I listened with a joyful heart; certainly God is faithful!

The book of Esther shows that God brings justice in his time and in his way. Sometimes the justice comes in the way we have expected, and at other times we are surprised by God's ways. But one thing remains certain. It is that God is faithful. He will provide and care for his people. From an overwhelming opposition to the smallest concern, God continues to be faithful to us. God provides not only for Esther and Mordecai, but for all of his people. Because he has been faithful, the people respond with rejoicing and celebrating. Our response to God should be no different.

---

1. Describe a time when God has proven himself faithful to you in a difficult situation.

2. Read chapter 8. List all the ways that Esther and Mordecai are rewarded by God through the actions of the king.

---

3. In verses 3-6 we see a little of Esther's heart. How does she feel toward her people?

---

4. What do verses 3-6 reveal about Esther's character?

---

5. Esther felt deep concern and compassion for her people. For what person or group of people would you like to have that same kind of concern?

How might you develop your compassion for them?

---

6. How does King Xerxes respond to Esther's plea (vv. 7-10)?

---

7. God provides for the Jews through the edict Mordecai issued in the king's name. How did the edict (vv. 11-13) provide what Esther was asking for in verses 5-6 without breaking the first edict (3:12-14)?

---

8. What is the response of the Jews to God's provision and protection (vv. 15-17)?

---

9. How did the response of the Jews to the first edict in chapter 4 (4:1-3, 15-16) pave the way for the events of this chapter?

---

10. How can we be faithful when we are waiting for God to act in our lives?

---

11. Think over the past week and share how God has been faithful to you. What is one way you can express to God your joy and gladness about his provision for you?

9
Remembering and Celebrating

Esther 9—10

It was a beautiful spring day and I was walking along a dirt road that wound through the mountains outside Bear Trap Ranch in Colorado. I was pouring out my heart to God and wrestling with where he wanted to take me in my life. As I strolled among the pine trees, God opened my eyes to the abundant life that lay before me if I would commit my future to his service. It was that moment that changed the course of my life, and I am eternally grateful to the Lord. Every time I visit Bear Trap Ranch I walk along that very road and remember that moment and God's faithfulness to me. Remembering helps me keep my perspective and empowers me to go on in my commitment to his service.

When God does something in our midst it is important to remember it and to celebrate. As we recollect his goodness, our faith is strengthened and so is our ability to face the next struggle.

---

1. What is something you or your family commemorated, and how was it celebrated?

2. Read Esther 9—10. Summarize the events of the thirteenth, fourteenth and fifteenth days of Adar.

---

3. Describe the people that the Jews actually destroyed on these days in the month of Adar (9:5-17).

---

4. The author mentions three separate times that the Jews did not lay their hands on their enemies' plunder. Why might the Jews have left the plunder despite the king's permission to take it (9:10, 15-16)?

---

5. Mordecai and Esther proclaimed and established the celebration of Purim as a holiday for all the Jews. What was the purpose of the celebration (vv. 20-27)?

---

6. The wording in verse 28 emphasizes the importance of the celebration for all the Jews. Why is the observation of Purim so crucial?

---

7. How were the Jews instructed to celebrate Purim (9:22)?

8. How is the celebration of Purim different from most of our celebrations?

---

9. God has saved his people and blessed Esther and Mordecai for their obedience to him. Summarize what happens to Esther and Mordecai at the end of the story (9:29—10:3).

---

10. What qualities did Mordecai have that made him a respected leader?

---

11. Throughout Scripture God instructs his people to commemorate the times when he acted to provide for and save his people. Why is remembering God's acts of faithfulness important for us as Christians?

---

12. What is one thing that God has done for you that you would truly like to remember?

What are some ways you could celebrate it?

Leader's Notes

Leading a Bible discussion can be an enjoyable and rewarding experience. But it can also be *scary*—especially if you've never done it before. If this is your feeling, you're in good company. When God asked Moses to lead the Israelites out of Egypt, he replied, "O Lord, please send someone else to do it!" (Ex 4:13).

When Solomon became king of Israel, he felt the task was beyond his abilities. "I am only a little child and do not know how to carry out my duties. . . . Who is able to govern this great people of yours?" (1 Kings 3:7, 9).

When God called Jeremiah to be a prophet, he replied, "Ah, Sovereign LORD, . . . I do not know how to speak; I am only a child" (Jer 1:6).

The list goes on. The apostles were "unschooled, ordinary men" (Acts 4:13). Timothy was young, frail and frightened. Paul's "thorn in the flesh" made him feel weak. But God's response to all of his servants—including you—is essentially the same: "My grace is sufficient for you" (2 Cor 12:9). Relax. God helped these people in spite of their weaknesses, and he can help you in spite of your feelings of inadequacy.

There is another reason why you should feel encouraged. Leading a Bible discussion is not difficult if you follow certain guidelines. You don't need to be an expert on the Bible or a trained teacher. The suggestions listed below should enable you to effectively and enjoyably fulfill your role as leader.

Preparing to Lead

1. Ask God to help you understand and apply the passage to your own life. Unless this happens, you will not be prepared to lead others. Pray too for the various members of the group. Ask God to give you an enjoyable and profitable time together studying his Word.

2. As you begin each study, read and reread the assigned Bible passage to familiarize yourself with what the author is saying. In the case of book studies, you may want to read through the entire book prior to the first study. This will give you a helpful overview of its contents.

3. This study guide is based on the New International Version of the Bible. It will help you and the group if you use this translation as the basis for your study and discussion. Encourage others to use the NIV also, but allow them the freedom to use whatever translation they prefer.

4. Carefully work through each question in the study. Spend time in meditation and reflection as you formulate your answers.

5. Write your answers in the space provided in the study guide. This will help you to express your understanding of the passage clearly.

6. It might help you to have a Bible dictionary handy. Use it to look up any unfamiliar words, names or places. (For additional help on how to study a passage, see chapter five of *Leading Bible Study Discussions*, SU).

7. Once you have finished your own study of the passage, familiarize yourself with the leader's notes for the study you are leading. These are designed to help you in several ways. First, they tell you the purpose the study guide author had in mind while writing the study. Take time to think through how the study questions work together to accomplish that purpose. Second, the notes provide you with additional background information or comments on some of the questions. This information can be useful if people have difficulty understanding or answering a question. Third, the leader's notes can alert you to potential problems you may encounter during the study.

8. If you wish to remind yourself of anything mentioned in the leader's notes, make a note to yourself below that question in the study.

Leading the Study

1. Begin the study on time. Unless you are leading an evangelistic Bible study, open with prayer, asking God to help you to understand and apply the passage.

2. Be sure that everyone in your group has a study guide. Encourage them to prepare beforehand for each discussion by working through the questions in the guide.

3. At the beginning of your first time together, explain that these studies are meant to be discussions not lectures. Encourage the members of the group to participate. However, do not put pressure on those who may be hesitant to speak during the first few sessions.

4. Read the introductory paragraph at the beginning of the discussion. This will orient the group to the passage being studied.

5. Read the passage aloud if you are studying one chapter or less. You may choose to do this yourself, or someone else may read if he or she has been asked to do so prior to the study. Longer passages may occasionally be read in parts at different times during the study. Some studies may cover several chapters. In such cases reading aloud would probably take too much time, so the group members should simply read the assigned passages prior to the study.

6. As you begin to ask the questions in the guide, keep several things in mind. First, the questions are designed to be used just as they are written. If you wish, you may simply read them aloud to the group. Or you may prefer to express them in your own words. However, unnecessary rewording of the questions is not recommended.

Second, the questions are intended to guide the group toward understanding and applying the *main idea* of the passage. The author of the guide has stated his or her view of this central idea in the *purpose* of the study in the leader's notes. You should try to understand how the passage expresses this idea and how the study questions work together to lead the group in that direction.

There may be times when it is appropriate to deviate from the study guide. For example, a question may have already been answered. If so, move on to the next question. Or someone may raise an important question not covered in the guide. Take time to discuss it! The important thing is to use discretion. There may be many routes you can travel to reach the goal of the study. But the easiest route is usually the one the author has suggested.

7. Avoid answering your own questions. If necessary, repeat or rephrase them until they are clearly understood. An eager group quickly becomes passive and silent if they think the leader will do most of the talking.

8. Don't be afraid of silence. People may need time to think about the question before formulating their answers.

9. Don't be content with just one answer. Ask, "What do the rest of you think?" or "Anything else?" until several people have given answers to the question.

10. Acknowledge all contributions. Try to be affirming whenever possible. Never reject an answer. If it is clearly wrong, ask, "Which verse led you to that conclusion?" or again, "What do the rest of you think?"

11. Don't expect every answer to be addressed to you, even though this will probably happen at first. As group members become more at ease, they will begin to truly interact with each other. This is one sign of a healthy discussion.

12. Don't be afraid of controversy. It can be very stimulating. If you don't resolve an issue completely, don't be frustrated. Move on and keep it in mind for later. A subsequent study may solve the problem.

13. Stick to the passage under consideration. It should be the source for answering the questions. Discourage the group from unnecessary cross-referencing. Likewise, stick to the subject and avoid going off on tangents.

14. Periodically summarize what the *group* has said about the passage. This helps to draw together the various ideas mentioned and gives continuity to the study. But don't preach.

15. Conclude your time together with conversational prayer. Be sure to ask God's help to apply those things which you learned in the study.

16. End on time.

Many more suggestions and helps are found in *Leading Bible Study Discussions* (SU). Reading and studying through that would be well worth your time.

Components of Small Groups

A healthy small group should do more than study the Bible. There are four components you should consider as you structure your time together.

Nurture. Being a part of a small group should be a nurturing and edifying experience. You should grow in your knowledge and love of God and each other. If we are to properly love God, we must know and keep his commandments (Jn 14:15). That is why Bible study should be a foundational part of your small group. But you can be nurtured by other things as well. You can memorize Scripture, read and discuss a book, or occasionally listen to a tape of a good speaker.

Community. Most people have a need for close friendships. Your small group can be an excellent place to cultivate such relationships. Allow time for informal interaction before and after the study. Have a time of sharing during the meeting. Do fun things together as a group, such as a potluck supper or a picnic. Have someone bring refreshments to the meeting. Be creative!

Worship. A portion of your time together can be spent in worship and prayer. Praise God together for who he is. Thank him for what he has done and is doing in your lives and in the world. Pray for each other's needs. Ask God to help you to apply what you have learned. Sing hymns together.

Mission. Many small groups decide to work together in some form of outreach. This can be a practical way of applying what you have learned. You can host a series of evangelistic discussions for your friends or neighbors. You can visit people at a home for the elderly. Help a widow with cleaning or repair jobs around her home. Such projects can have a transforming influence on your group.

For a detailed discussion of the nature and function of small groups, read *Small Group Starter Kit* or *Growing Christians in Small Groups* (both from IVP).

Study 1. A Little Respect. Esther 1.

Purpose: To show that respect between individuals is built through mutual regard and appreciation rather than through demanding respect or controlling one another.

Question 1. Every study begins with an "approach" question, which is meant to be asked before the passage is read. These questions are important for several reasons.

First, they help the group to warm up to each other. No matter how well a group may know each other, there is always a stiffness that needs to be overcome before people will begin to talk openly. A good question will break the ice.

Second, approach questions get people thinking along the lines of the topic of the study. Most people will have lots of different things going on in their minds (dinner, an important meeting coming up, how to get the car fixed) that will have nothing to do with the study. A creative question will get their attention and draw them into the discussion.

Third, approach questions can reveal where our thoughts or feelings need to be transformed by Scripture. That is why it is especially important not to read the passage before the approach question is asked. The passage will tend to color the honest reactions people would otherwise give because they are, of course, supposed to think the way the Bible does. Giving honest responses before they find out what the Bible says may help them see where their thoughts or attitudes need to be changed.

Question 2. This is a survey question for the chapter. It introduces all the different people that are a part of this initial scene. Noticing all the characters will provide an overview of the events as well.

Besides naming the main characters, such as King Xerxes and Queen Vashti, make sure the group names the nobles, officials, military leaders, princes, people from the citadel of Susa, the wives of these guests, the eunuchs and the wise men. Being aware of who was invited to the party will help the group in answering some of the other questions.

Question 3. The author spends several verses describing the details of this celebration—the furnishings, the guests, the decorations and the abundant wine. The length of the celebration is also important. King Xerxes may have wanted to display his great wealth and power to the nobles and officials he had invited. It is likely that he took this opportunity to present his plans to attack Greece and to plan the campaigns with his military leaders. (King Xerxes carried out his plans against Greece in 481 B.C.) If this was the case, King Xerxes may have been trying to show his guests his authority and power in the kingdom and his credibility in preparation for his Greek campaigns.

Everyone would certainly have been impressed by the king's wealth and power.

Question 4. It is important to the development of the study to spend some time discussing why King Xerxes made such a request of the queen. Help the group see how the scene has been set by the celebration. Note how the wine and the party may have led to such a request. The king has displayed all of his wealth and possessions and now desires to display his most beautiful treasure. His motive seems to have been to impress his guests further by showing off his wife's beauty.

Question 5. It will be important for you to aid the group in seeing all aspects of Vashti's predicament. The request is not a noble one. The king wants her to appear in front of his drunken guests only to display herself. To obey the request would mean degrading herself in front of the guests. At the same time, refusing to obey the king's command would most certainly bring about serious consequences. Her disobedience, especially in front of the people the king was trying to impress, would place Xerxes in an awkward position as well. His authority would be questioned. It is unlikely that Vashti would have refused the king without careful thought. She must have felt strongly enough about the situation to risk the consequences for disobedience.

Vashti's decision is an important element in the book. Because of Vashti's refusal, there will be a search for a new queen, which allows Esther to enter the story and save her people. Help the group see themselves in her position and wrestle with what to decide.

Question 6. Even though we have only a few verses so far on which to make observations about the king's character, it is possible to make some initial comments. Because of his extravagance and the nature of his request to Vashti, King Xerxes seems to be a man caught up in his own wealth and power. He appears to be a prideful man whose worth rests in praise and recognition from others and in his possessions. Further, in his request of the queen, King Xerxes shows that he doesn't respect Queen Vashti as a person.

Question 9. Although the wise men were honest, and certainly a respect for authority is healthy, the wise men viewed respect as something that was demanded and gained through forced obedience, not mutual respect and appreciation.

Question 10. If respect develops between people, it is because there is mutual regard and appreciation. The dictionary tells us that respect involves showing esteem, consideration and honor for the other person. This is the point where you can direct the group back to their answers to the first question. Discussing why they respect someone should help them determine how respect is gained.

Study 2. Trusting God's Work. Esther 2.

Purpose: To recognize God's ordering work in our lives and to trust his direction.

Question 2. Note that four years have passed since Queen Vashti was dethroned. Compare 2:16, which cites the seventh year of King Xerxes' reign, and 1:2, which takes place in the third year of King Xerxes' reign. During the time between Vashti's disposal and the events in chapter 2 King Xerxes was occupied with his military campaigns in Greece. It was after his defeat in 479 B.C. that he returned to Susa and remembered what had happened to Vashti.

Question 4. The purpose of these women and the harem in general was to provide pleasure to the king. They had no rights and their lives were restricted and probably very dull. They remained in the harem until they were called by name by the king (v. 12). If they were called, they would go to the king to give him sexual pleasure. The women who were not crowned queen would most likely live out their lives much like widows (v. 14). If Esther had not been chosen, she would have become one of those women forgotten by the king.

In the discussion of question 7 the group can begin to see how Esther's role does change, and therefore how she is in a better position to help her people. Again in question 10 this concept will appear as one of the circumstances God orchestrates to accomplish his plans.

Question 5. Esther won favor with Hegai, all those who saw her and the king. She was indeed beautiful. However, Esther showed other appealing qualities. It seems that Esther would not have won everyone's approval if it was only physical beauty that she possessed. Esther's presence, demeanor and personality must have been part of her appeal.

Each woman that was ready to appear before the king was offered anything she wanted to take with her. She could have requested jewels, clothing, cosmetics or other ornaments to enhance her beauty and her chance of being chosen. Esther chose only those things that Hegai suggested. Certainly her humility and modesty would have shown.

In studying character throughout this book you'll find that a person's character and presence affects others and is appealing—or repelling. How people view us says a lot about our character.

Question 7. This question is really the second part of question 4. Because Esther was the queen, she had more rights, freedom, influence and authority than the other women. She was in a position where she could accomplish more for God when the time came.

Question 9. We have not seen a tremendous amount of Mordecai yet in the story, but just as the plot of a movie unfolds scene after scene, more and more about a person's character can be observed with each glimpse into that person's life. Mordecai displays integrity in his choice to reveal the assassination plot against the king even though there may be risks involved. Mordecai also shows some deep concern for Esther by continuing to seek out information about her. He does not leave her in the palace and forget about her, but instead goes to visit each day.

People put together a picture of our character from the times they interact with us, no matter how briefly. God wants us to be people of godly, consistent character, and that means choosing to do what is right in all situations.

Question 10. Guide the group in looking at the many ways God has been at work to set things in place: Esther's being blessed with extraordinary beauty, Mordecai's being employed at the king's gate so that he hears the assassination plot, Queen Vashti's refusal in the first chapter which leads to the search for a new queen, God's working in the hearts and minds of those Esther encounters so that she wins their approval, and Mordecai's name and deed being recorded in the annals of the king. The group will begin to see how God is orchestrating events and circumstances so that everything will be in place when the threat from Haman surfaces. As you work through the study guide, help the group to see how God does this throughout the whole book.

Study 3. Evaluating Advice. Esther 3.

Purpose: To discover how to evaluate the counsel we receive from others and to give good advice.

Question 3. The conflict between Mordecai and Haman begins with Mordecai's refusing to honor Haman by bowing down to him. Although this initiates the conflict, the history between Mordecai's people, the Jews, and Haman's people, the Amalekites, intensifies the problem. The Jewish people bowed before kings and other people at times throughout their history to show honor and respect (1 Sam 24:8; 1 Kings 1:16; Gen 33:3). So the reason Mordecai refused to honor Haman in this way was probably not because he felt he would be worshiping Haman as a god. The reason stems from the intense rivalry between the Amalekites and the Jews.

It will be necessary to review the story of the conflict before moving on in the study. The leader can summarize the story or the group may look up the relevant passages and read about the history themselves. It is important to know the story because the reason that Haman's response to Mordecai is so intense is because of the long-standing conflict between their peoples. This will help the group understand Haman and Mordecai much better. The Scriptures to which you can direct the group are Exodus 17:8-15, Deuteronomy 25:17-19 and 1 Samuel 15:1-9.

Questions 4-5. Verses 8-9 are fascinating! Help the group to look closely at the way Haman approaches the subject, how he manipulates the king and appeals to Xerxes' greed and desire for power. For example, Haman knows that his offer of money will appeal to the king. He also knows that the king will not like the idea that there are people in his kingdom who challenge his authority by not obeying his rule. The Jews did in fact have their own customs, but they were obedient to the king and did not cause any trouble in the kingdom. Furthermore, Haman is careful not to reveal the name of the people he wants destroyed or that his motivation for their destruction comes from his own personal anger. In fact, Haman comes across as a concerned subject wishing to protect the king and to act in the king's best interest. Haman weaves a tapestry of truth, half-truths and lies in order to convince the king of his plan.

It will be easy for the group to see Haman's manipulation and deceit in this chapter. However, question 5 will give them a chance to see how easily we can act in the same ways. Guide the group in relating experiences where it was tempting for them to try to manipulate another for their gain or to stretch the truth so they appear to be doing the right thing. We are frequently guilty of the very same things as Haman.

Question 7. The author uses repetition of words such as *each*, *every* and *all* to emphasize the intensity of the threat against the Jews. The author also spends several verses describing how and where the edict was issued. The detail and repetition set the scene for the reader. The edict would touch the life of every Jew; no one would be missed. The threat against them was overwhelming and all-encompassing.

Question 9. King Xerxes shows more of his prideful and greedy character by the way he is so easily convinced to destroy a whole group of people because of greed and pride. Several commentaries believe that the king did accept the money Haman offered and that the refusal was merely politeness and custom. The last verse of this chapter reveals even more about Xerxes. He and Haman sit down to drink totally unconcerned about the people whose destruction they have ordered. He shows a lack of concern or compassion.

Question 10. You may want to refer back to the introduction and the quote from Tozer. Help the group think through the ways that we give unwise advice and how to keep ourselves from falling into those patterns. It is crucial that before we offer counsel we are willing to seek the Lord for his wisdom and insight about the situation, but also that we are willing to hear the Lord speak about things in our own lives. We must remain humble before God and others when giving advice.

Question 11. Be sure to allow enough time for a good discussion of this question. It is easy for us to be swayed by others and to act on the counsel of others even when the advice is poor. Seeking the Lord's wisdom, speaking to several people, comparing the advice with Scripture and being selective with the people you choose to seek counsel from are several ways you can evaluate advice. Help the group wrestle with the necessity to evaluate any counsel they receive.

Study 4. Doing the Right Thing. Esther 4.

Purpose: To recognize the situations in which God has placed you to do his will and commit to acting with courage and integrity in those situations.

Question 3. Mordecai responded to the news about the edict by tearing his clothes, putting on sackcloth and ashes, and mourning. He was grieving in every way possible. He was publicly displaying his grief about the situation by wailing through the city streets.

The Jews responded in the same ways as Mordecai. There was great mourning, fasting, weeping and wailing. It is important to note that in every place the edict went there was the same reaction. This is a strong example of community and the connectedness of the Jews as a people.

The Jews wore sackcloth and ashes when mourning and in hopes of averting national catastrophe. Help the group see that the Jews immediately turned to their God for help. They sought God's protection and mercy before doing anything else. This sometimes is not our first response to tragic news.

Question 4. There has been great feasting and celebrating in the book so far (1:3, 4-8, 9; 2:18; 3:15). Haman and the king sit down for a drink, which seems to be a joyful, relaxed situation. Help the group to see the contrast between their feasting and the mourning of the Jewish people. It seems that the fate of a whole people has been determined by these two men, but in reality the fate of the Jews remains with the sovereign God.

Question 5. Mordecai is aware of the influential position Esther holds as the queen. He realizes the potential she has in affecting this situation. He also knows that God has placed her in this position for a reason, and he reveals that to Esther in verse 14. Mordecai pleads with Esther because she is the only one who has access to the king.

Questions 6-7. Esther first reacts by thinking about the risks she personally faces in going to the king. If a person approaches the king without being summoned, that person is in danger of being put to death unless the king gives a pardon. At this point Esther is not thinking about helping her people or using her position to influence the fate of the Jews. She is probably afraid, nervous and uncertain when she receives Mordecai's first message.

This question will hopefully lead the group to see that Esther did experience some of the same feelings that we experience when we are faced with something difficult. Question 8 allows the group to expand on their own reactions and feelings when God called them to carry out his will in a certain situation. It is helpful to know that Esther thinks about her own safety first because it highlights her final decision to carry out Mordecai's instructions. The fact that she was afraid but had the courage and character to go through with it anyway is motivating.

Question 9. Mordecai's arguments highlight some very important principles for Esther. He reminds her that there are consequences for failing to do what God asks. If Esther refuses to help her people, she will be a victim of Haman's plot as well. Mordecai also persuades her by helping her to see the divine intervention in her becoming the queen so that she would be in a position to help her people when the time came.

This is a very important concept for the group to touch on because it reminds us that God does place us in relationships, jobs or locations for a reason.

Question 10. The themes of the book of Esther are seen most clearly in this chapter. The relationship between God's sovereign working in the world and the response of his people is witnessed in Mordecai's arguments. Mordecai is convinced that God will still provide deliverance for the Jews even if Esther refuses to go to the king. God will not abandon his chosen people by letting them be completely destroyed. This is God's sovereignty. He is ultimately in control, and he will accomplish his plans.

However, he chooses to work through his people. If Esther decides to go to the king and plead for her people, she will be used by God and experience the privilege of being part of the plan. If she chooses not to help, she will not keep God's plan from happening, she will only experience consequences for her action and miss out on the opportunity God gave her.

Again, it is important to help the group touch on this relationship. As they think through this in context of Esther's situation, hopefully they will realize that God will accomplish his plans in their lives, but that they do have a choice to be involved or to experience the consequences.

Question 11. The key character qualities that Esther shows are courage, a dependence on God and moral strength. This is a good time to touch on verse 16, which shows that Esther turned to her people for support and that she knew she must turn to God in order to be able to face the risks.

Study 5. The Heart of the Matter. Esther 5.

Purpose: To guard against facing difficult times or tasks with anger or bitterness and learn to face them with humility and a dependence on God.

Question 2. Esther not only risks going before the king, but also delays answering him twice. She appears before him unsummoned, which could bring about her immediate death if the king does not extend a pardon. Esther does not know how the king will respond to her or to her delays in stating her request. Another aspect here is the plight of her people if she meets with death. Who will help them if she cannot?

Question 4. Chapter 3 talks about the fasting that Esther requested of her people and that she fasted as well. Prayer usually accompanies such fasting. It seems consistent that her people were spending time fasting and interceding for her. Esther was no doubt deep in prayer at this point also. The prayers and fasting gave Esther strength and courage to carry out her plan. The recognition that God may have placed her in the position of queen for this specific purpose might have spurred her on as well.

Help the group talk about the ways Esther was strengthened and empowered, so that the group members will be reminded that we all desperately need the prayers and support of our friends and family in order to fulfill God's call and to develop consistent character.

Question 6. The reason Esther makes this request is not specifically stated, but it is probable that in her times of fasting and prayer she felt God was instructing her to wait and to approach the king in this way. Asking for two separate banquets also might have conveyed to the king the importance of her request. The delay in stating the request allowed for other events such as Mordecai's involvement in the assassination plot and Haman's gallows to surface. Another motivation for Esther may have been the atmosphere of the court in comparison with the atmosphere of a banquet. There were no doubt many attendants and others in the court, and there would have been fewer people at a banquet just for the king and Haman. She may have felt it more appropriate to plead for her life and for her people in the banquet setting.

It is important for the group to see that the Jews and Esther prayed and fasted before she made her careful plans. How often we take action without seeking the Lord or the advice and support of our Christian community.

Question 7. Esther uses words that reveal her to be a person of humility. She seeks to please and to honor the king. Esther's actions shout the condition of her heart, but her actual words reveal much as well about who she is. As Jesus says in Matthew 12:34, "For out of the overflow of the heart the mouth speaks."

Question 8. Haman was an arrogant man who measured his worth based on his power and influence over others. His desire to control others and receive honor was his goal. He was controlled by his anger, bitterness and pride.

Question 9. Haman was consumed with a racial hatred for the Jews, but his personal hatred for Mordecai stemmed from Mordecai's refusal to honor him. Mordecai's refusal challenged Haman's power and his self-centredness. His pride was attacked by Mordecai, and he was not appreciated or honored as he felt he should be.

Haman's hatred soured his life to the point that he could not enjoy anything. The list of things that Haman boasted about held no joy for him because of the one thing he hated desperately—Mordecai. Hatred and bitterness in our lives will produce the same effects. Bitterness will sour everything and return again and again until it is dealt with.

Question 10. The issue of doing what is right stands out in this question. Esther had courage and humility and acted in the way that was right. She risked everything for God and her people, and Haman acted only for evil and self-interest.

Study 6. Recognizing Unrighteousness. Esther 6.

Purpose: To identify those areas of our character which are displeasing to God and to present those before him, asking him to rid us of these traits.

Question 2. The book of Esther is full of examples about God's working through circumstances to bring about his purposes. This chapter has plenty of seemingly coincidental incidents that again show us that God is in control and is working everything out for his good. The king *happens* to have trouble sleeping that night and *happens* to read the exact section of the book of the annals which recorded Mordecai's good deed. At the same time Haman *happens* to be in the court when the king decides to honor Mordecai and he ends up being the one who must honor Mordecai. God uses insignificant things to his glory and for his plans. This is a major theme in the book and is seen very clearly in this chapter.

Question 4. The construction of this book is incredible. The author uses repetition, irony, contrast and humor to communicate the story. It will be helpful to the group if they can see some of the irony contained in the story. The king, on this particular night, is preoccupied with how to honor someone who has done a good deed and has gone without recognition for five years. His intentions on this night were to honor. Haman's intentions were to destroy. He has also spent the night awake; however, he has occupied himself by building gallows on which to execute Mordecai. It is ironic that the very person both men are thinking about is Mordecai. Adding to the irony is the fact that Haman enters the court to approach the king about executing Mordecai, but he has no idea that he will leave the court to honor his adversary in front of the whole city.

Question 6. At this point have the group summarize the things they have already seen in Haman's character. The observations made in this question will add to the portrait. Help the group look through these three verses and discuss the motivations for suggesting such a reward.

Haman was already wealthy, but he desired popularity and recognition. He was obsessed with prestige. Haman did not suggest giving the honored man money or jewels, because he craved public acclaim. Again Haman's pride and arrogance are revealed.

Question 8. The response of Haman's wife and friends provides some interesting insight. First, Zeresh affirms Haman's downfall. Perhaps she realized the power of the God of the Jews, or she recognized the perseverance of the people through so much. Perhaps she was acknowledging the ultimate victory of the Jews over the Amalekites. But whatever the reason, she provides a gloomy picture. Second, Zeresh and the friends in essence abandon Haman. They initially suggested building the gallows but now leave all the responsibility in the hands of Haman.

Even their language indicates their abandonment of Haman. They say *you* or *your* three times in one sentence. They are assuming no part in his humiliation or downfall.

Question 9. This is an important question for the group to discuss because it leads into the application questions. Haman's pride and desire for recognition worked against him to place him in a very humiliating situation. The people in Susa would have known about the rivalry between Mordecai and Haman because of Mordecai's refusal to bow down to him at the king's gate. In this way Haman suffered the consequences of unrighteousness in his life.

We too fall prey to our unrighteousness. We can be prideful, hateful, impatient, unloving and so on. And there are many times when we act according to our sinful nature. We then suffer the consequences, whether they be broken relationships, physical tragedy or unrest in our hearts.

Study 7. Character No Matter What. Esther 7.

Purpose: To commit to doing what is right whether or not we experience justice in this life.

Question 2. This is the point in the story where everything comes out in the open. The truth is no longer hidden but is laid out for all to see and experience. Esther's nationality is revealed to the king and to Haman. King Xerxes finds out the identity of the people group Haman has coerced him into destroying. Esther and Xerxes discover that Haman has built a gallows for Mordecai's execution, and Haman's true character is most clearly revealed to the king. The scene depicts what Jesus talked about in John 3—those whose deeds are evil love darkness. Haman kept a lot of things secret, but when they were brought into the light they caused his downfall.

This chapter is a good reminder to us that our evil deeds will come to light in the end—and often in this life—and we will face the consequences of those deeds.

Question 3. This question will help the group to summarize what has happened in the previous chapters. Each person has been dealing with different emotions and circumstances up to this point, and it will be interesting for the group members to try to put themselves in the characters' shoes at this point.

Esther knows the king will ask about her request, and she will have to ask for his mercy. She will be revealing her nationality with no idea of how the news will be received. She also does not know if the king will do anything to spare her people. She may be feeling nervous and anxious about the outcome of the evening. Haman is obsessed with Mordecai and is consumed with anger toward him. He has also just been through a very humiliating experience in front of the whole city. He is probably fuming and embarrassed. The king, on the other hand, has no knowledge of either Esther's situation or Haman's anger. He perhaps is curious to know Esther's request; he is enjoying himself at the banquet and relaxing over wine.

Question 4. There is a great deal contained in these two verses. Guide the group through each part of Esther's request so they will be able to see how she handles herself before the king. This gives some more insight into her character as well. Esther begins her request with politeness and courtesy. She asks the king if she has found favor. She states her request very plainly, perhaps indicating her desperation. Her first request would have revealed her identity and would have taken Xerxes by surprise, but she quickly proceeds to plead for her people, not just herself. She describes the threat against her people by using the exact words of the edict.

There is some question about the meaning of her last statement. The group might wrestle with how Esther could have thought being sold into slavery was not worthy of bothering the king. However, there are two ways of looking at her comment. One is that she was making reference to the king's financial concerns, and that the destruction of the Jews would be a loss to him. The other possibility is that she felt that to bother the king with a request was a serious undertaking, and the selling of her people would not have been serious enough to bother him.

Question 5. Many of their thoughts and emotions may come up in the answers to other questions, but it is good to have the group again put themselves into the shoes of the characters. It will help them interact with the passage more deeply.

King Xerxes is surprised at the nationality of his wife and horrified that he has played a part in the plotting against her people. It is his official seal which finalized the edict which ordered their destruction. He is extremely angry with Haman for manipulating him and coercing him into this situation. His reaction is to leave for the garden, taking time to decide on the punishment or to cool down enough to even speak. Haman is terrified because everything has been reversed for him in a matter of minutes. He has discovered that his plan threatened the life of the queen, and he realizes his life is now in danger.

Question 6. Noting the irony allows the group to see how masterfully the author communicated the story. It is ironic that Haman is uncovered by a Jew, a member of his enemies. It is ironic that he must beg Esther, a Jew, for his life and that his life comes to an end on the very gallows that he built to end the life of his adversary. Haman believed he would be honored, and now he faces death. Esther believed she might die, but now she will be honored.

Question 7. Haman's response is to beg the queen for mercy. He knows that his only chance is to approach Esther and ask for grace. In so doing he breaks a very strict rule of court etiquette. To approach the queen and speak to her without the king present was to cause great offense. He risked it in order to try one last plea for his life. His timing was horrible, and his fate was sealed.

The group might have difficulty delving this deeply into the reactions of Xerxes and Haman, so keep reminding them of all the truths that have now

come out and ask them how each man would have reacted to each revelation.
Question 9. This is a key question because it brings together the passage and our experience in life. We see in the passage justice being carried out. The wicked are punished, but the righteous are rewarded. Those who have integrity and godly character triumph. But in our experience this is not always what happens. We choose to do what is right but are not rewarded; sometimes our situations become worse because of our choices. Our motivation for doing what is right is in understanding that justice will ultimately occur. We may not witness justice in this life, but we know from Scripture that justice will be done. Psalm 73 reminds us that when we are frustrated with the lack of justice, we must go to the sanctuary of God for his perspective. We must continue to do what is right whether or not justice happens now.

Study 8. Praising God's Faithfulness. Esther 8.
Purpose: To be aware of God's faithfulness in our lives and continually praise him for it.
Question 2. This is an overview question which helps the group see how God provided for Mordecai and Esther. King Xerxes awards the estate of Haman to Esther. The estate of a person, that is, everything that a person owned, was reverted to the throne when that person became a condemned criminal. So all of Haman's belongings became Xerxes', which he then presented to Esther as compensation for the plot against her. Mordecai was first of all brought into the court, then given the position of manager of Haman's estate. He was given Xerxes' signet ring, which signified his legal authority to act in the king's name. Look throughout the whole chapter, because even in the last few verses we see more of Mordecai's rewards. In verse 15 we see Mordecai dressed in royal colors and royal robes, which demonstrated his position as second only to the king himself.

This is a good place to discuss the relationship between doing what is right and receiving rewards on earth. In the book of Esther, Mordecai and Esther faithfully serve God and do what is right. They receive earthly rewards. However, in our lives we must be careful not to let our motivation for choosing to do what is right be earthly rewards. They may come and they may not. God does not promise that we will receive rewards here on earth for our service to him. Our motivation should be our love for God and for others and our desire to be Christlike.
Questions 3-4. Esther is still grieving even though she has received many rewards. She has not forgotten the plight of her people. The horrible plot against the Jews is still in motion, and so she must go to the king once more.

She expresses her deep love, compassion and concern for her people through her weeping, begging and pleading before the king. She is connected with them; they are her own people. Her heart will not rest until there is relief for them.

Esther shows her true character in these few verses. She shows that she is not self-seeking. Her motivation for approaching the king initially is not out of concern for her own well-being. Her heart is for her people.

We fail so frequently in feeling this deeply for those around us. We are so often seeking our own comfort and security that we miss the suffering of others. Do we feel so connected with other people or other Christians that we seek out ways of relieving their plight? Would we risk our security, our lives for them?

Question 6. First of all, King Xerxes reminds Esther and Mordecai of what he has done for them already. But he does not stop at just rewarding them. He agrees to put a stop to the edict Haman instigated. He agrees to grant Esther's plea. However, the first edict cannot be repealed. Once an edict was issued it could not be altered or revoked. The only way left for him to thwart the first edict was to allow a second one that would in some way minimize or offset the effects of the first. King Xerxes gave Mordecai the permission and the authority to issue a second edict as he saw fit. The king put at Mordecai's disposal the translators and secretaries of the court to work on the edict as well as the fastest horses in the kingdom to carry the edict as quickly as possible.

Question 7. Mordecai attempted to construct an edict that would offset the effects of the initial order. The initial edict allowed the enemies of the Jews to destroy, kill and annihilate them on one particular day. So Mordecai issued an edict that allowed the Jews to gather together and protect themselves against this attack. They could kill those who sought to destroy them and plunder their property. Commentators differ on their opinions about this edict. Some say that the Jews were encouraged to seek revenge and to attack any of their enemies without boundaries. Others hold the view that the Jews were instructed to only defend themselves and their families. Thus, any killing that would occur would be in self-defense and not all-out revenge. This explanation seems likely and the NIV translation seems to indicate this in verse 11. It also appears unlikely that the king would have allowed an edict that would let the Jews attack the Persian people so overwhelmingly.

The group may discuss this, but it is important to help them focus on how the second edict would offset the first and how God provides the way out for his people. We want to focus on the Lord and his provision: the fact that the Jews faced incredible opposition and yet God protected and saved them. His faithfulness is paramount. He is faithful not only to Esther and Mordecai, who served him so obediently, but to all his people.

Question 9. Chapter 4 describes how the Jews responded to the first edict. There was great mourning, fasting and weeping. The Jews immediately turned to their God for his mercy and protection. They knew that their only hope was in God, so they prayed. In this chapter we see the results of God's acting to provide for them. Now they are filled with joy. There is great contrast in the responses, but they are connected. The Jews first turned to God. He answered their prayers, and they responded to his faithfulness with feasting and celebrating.

This should lead nicely into the application questions about our own responses to God when he cares for us.

Study 9. Remembering and Celebrating. Esther 9—10.

Purpose: To learn to become people of thanksgiving, celebrating in tangible, glorifying ways the times when God has provided for us.

Question 3. It is important to have the group look at what actually occurred during the days of destruction. As we read these last chapters of Esther, we are struck with what seems to be a great slaughter of people by the Jews. They seem to show little mercy to their enemies. Helping the group to focus on the text in answering this question will give some insight into the mindset of the Jews and into their motives.

The Jews acted in self-defense, attacking those who sought their destruction. There were boundaries to their actions. According to the text they apparently attacked only their enemies, only men, and only those who hated them. Question 4 adds further insight into their boundaries. It may be helpful to discuss verse 5, because the wording is somewhat difficult. It seems to imply that the Jews, following their human nature, did just what they wanted with their enemies, which is not a positive implication. However, the verse probably suggests that the Jews were free from any intervention on the part of the king's officials. This scene can be difficult for us to understand and may only truly be understood by those who have faced such persecution.

Question 4. Because the author mentions this three times, he obviously is trying to make a point. Several times in the history of the Jews the issue of taking their enemies' plunder surfaces. In Genesis 14:21-23 Abraham refuses the plunder from Sodom. Then later we witness Saul's descent from the favor of God because he takes plunder from his battle with the Amalekites. This incident was remembered by the Jewish people, and they refused to take the spoil even with King Xerxes' permission.

Ask the group what the Jews' refusing the plunder tells us about their motives in destroying their enemies. The Jews were not motivated by selfish gain or by enriching themselves personally with their enemies' property. They were not bent on a bloody revenge.

Question 6. The repetition of the word *every* emphasizes the importance of the Purim celebration to the Jews. It was something that everyone was to remember for all generations. The reason it was viewed as so crucial was because of the great saving act of God. The Jews as a people were saved from utter destruction. Their mourning was turned into joy by the goodness of God. Remembering would help them keep their perspective as to God's working in their lives as a people and would strengthen them in the face of other trials. Their celebration would be a rich fragrance to the Lord.

Questions 7-8. The Jews were instructed to celebrate by feasting, giving presents to each other and gifts to the poor. By giving gifts to one another, they emphasized the connectedness of the Jewish community, which experienced God's deliverance from Haman's plot. The gifts given to the poor were probably gifts of food so that those who were without the means to feast during Purim would be able to share the celebration. What a wonderful expression of community! The celebration of Purim helped to unite the people and encourage the whole community.

Direct the group in thinking through our own celebrations. Do we bring together the community, whether that be the body of Christ or families or small groups, through our celebrations? Do we focus on ourselves rather than recognizing those who are less fortunate? Are our celebrations of God's faithfulness glorifying to him, and do they help us to remember his mighty acts?

Questions 9-10. We can now put together some final observations about character. Esther is still concerned with her people. She is very active in the job of encouraging her people in the festival of Purim. She sees the value of the celebration and the benefits to the Jews. Mordecai remained unaffected by his place of power and prestige. In his position the temptation to become corrupt or work for personal gain may have been strong. Yet he strived for the good of the Jews, he spoke in their defense and for their welfare, and he was well received by the kingdom. This shows his strength of character and his high commitment to be a man of godly character.

Questions 11-12. If we desire to be people of godly character, we must recognize our need to remember and celebrate God's mighty acts. This glorifies the Lord and is a witness to those around us. Many times the apostle

Paul exhorts us to be thankful. We worship the Lord when our lives are characterized by giving thanks for who God is and for what he has done in our midst.

The concept of planning some kind of remembrance or celebration for a particular incident where God provided may be a new concept for many. Yet it would bring us together as the community of believers, enhance our thankfulness, and be a testimony to the world, especially if we included others in some way. Help the group to be specific in their answers. This might be an opportunity for the group as a whole to plan something to celebrate what God has done in the group. To commemorate your experience together with the Lord would be a fitting way to end your study of Esther.

Other ideas for concluding the Esther study with a group:

☐ The Jewish people still celebrate Purim today. One way to end the study may be to plan a traditional Purim celebration. Some of the things that are part of the celebration include feasting, hosting a costume ball where each person dresses as one of the characters from the book of Esther, and reading the book aloud while the partygoers cheer when Esther and Mordecai are mentioned and boo when Haman and others are mentioned.

☐ Plan a celebration where the group distributes gifts to each other and to those who are less fortunate.

Patty Pell is a staffworker with InterVarsity Christian Fellowship at the University of Northern Colorado. She and her husband, Scott, live with their daughter, Madeline, in Greeley, Colorado.

What Should We Study Next?

A good place to start your study of Scripture would be with a book study. Many groups begin with a Gospel such as *Mark* (22 studies by Jim Hoover) or *John* (26 studies by Douglas Connelly). These guides are divided into two parts so that if 22 or 26 weeks seems like too much to do at once, the group can feel free to do half and take a break with another topic. Later you might want to come back to it. You might prefer to try a shorter letter. *Philippians* (9 studies by Donald Baker), *Ephesians* (13 studies by Andrew T. and Phyllis J. Le Peau) and *1 & 2 Timothy and Titus* (12 studies by Pete Sommer) are good options. If you want to vary your reading with an Old Testament book, consider *Ecclesiastes* (12 studies by Bill and Teresa Syrios) for a challenging and exciting study.

There are a number of interesting topical LifeBuilder studies as well. Here are some options for filling three or four quarters of a year:

Basic Discipleship
Christian Beliefs, 12 studies by Stephen D. Eyre
Christian Character, 12 studies by Andrea Sterk & Peter Scazzero
Christian Disciplines, 12 studies by Andrea Sterk & Peter Scazzero
Evangelism, 12 studies by Rebecca Pippert & Ruth Siemens

Building Community
Christian Community, 12 studies by Rob Suggs
Fruit of the Spirit, 9 studies by Hazel Offner
Spiritual Gifts, 12 studies by Charles & Anne Hummel

Character Studies
New Testament Characters, 12 studies by Carolyn Nystrom
Old Testament Characters, 12 studies by Peter Scazzero
Old Testament Kings, 12 studies by Carolyn Nystrom
Women of the Old Testament, 12 studies by Gladys Hunt

The Trinity
Meeting God, 12 studies by J. I. Packer
Meeting Jesus, 13 studies by Leighton Ford
Meeting the Spirit, 12 studies by Douglas Connelly